TONI

≈ *in the* ≈

MEANTIME

A Care-Guide for Women Facing a Combative Divorce

FOREWORD

*"In the middle of the journey of our life
I found myself within a dark woods where
the straight way was lost."*

—DANTE ALIGHIERI, *Inferno*

Dear friend,

I wanted to give you a gift. Perhaps a little book. A little book that would support you during this challenging time. I wasn't looking for a 'how to' book. I didn't want a 'shelf help' book. I wouldn't want a 'what you need to know about the law' legal jargon book. I especially didn't want a 'what happens, should happen, and never happens' book. I simply wanted a little book. One that wouldn't take much time, one that would give you core wisdom to lift your spirits, remind you that you are not alone, and guide you back to yourself and to what's possible. A little book that will serve you in creating your own way up this mountain called your divorce.

I couldn't find one. So, I took the time to create one

myself, but not by myself. My true love and beloved husband helped me along the way. By my side, he loved, sourced, inspired and supported me in getting my best out on paper. In doing so, he also took upon himself all the rest, that which wasn't my best. The magnitude of what this entailed and the healing it provided to me cannot be captured in words. I will never be able to fully express my appreciation for his part in this book. Without him, I know now I wouldn't have had the strength or ability to retrace my own mountain solo, let alone return safely and intact. This journey back was the only way to fully glean the wisdom contained in this book. It required me to once again painfully face dreams that once were, unchangeable miss-steps and their resulting casualties, and the malicious betrayals of those once loved so dearly. These are best left in the past if not for a greater purpose to save others from similar, unnecessary heartbreak. Together, side by side, we made this journey to serve those of you who will read this book and find hope, strength and courage. To voice the truth in 12 myths from my own and others' similar experiences, from my gifts of observation and tools as a professional life coach, and from my love for all who are courageously willing to dare to keep climbing and to reach the top. This book is for all kindred spirits who climb similar mountaintops long after my footprints have faded from my own.

Here it is; the little book that may help and guide you

in the mean time. Please read it from the love and support of someone who did her best to fairly create, endure and complete her own steep mountain and reached the top. Mount Everest would have been easier it seems. I know first hand how difficult it may be. There is no map. What may be the right trail for someone else may not be the right one for you. What others think is in your best interest may not be what you know in your heart to be in yours. It can feel very isolating and overwhelming trying to find your own voice in the noise of everyone else's.

You can do it. Take heart and keep faith! This is our gift to you. May these following mean time myths and prudent principles serve you as a guide, as a North Star, as a compass on your mountain until you reach the top.

"Whoever cannot seek the unforeseen
sees nothing for the known way is an impasse."

~ HERACLITUS 475 B.C.

INTRODUCTION

This book is designed to lift your spirits and give you hope that it is possible to overcome the obstacles facing you in your necessary divorce. Specifically, I want to show you how to focus your lens on only that which you can control throughout this journey...yourself. This book will show you specific thoughts, beliefs and inherited discourses – 'myths' - that may have you trapped. One such myth you are likely to encounter is the belief that how you treat the other person will determine how they treat you in return. Another is that once the experts are involved it will get better. Exposing these 12 common myths will give you alternate possibilities and actions that can make the difference in your divorce.

Throughout this book I will ask you to look directly at unpleasant realities both in yourself and in others, not to make things worse but so that you can free yourself from what's ailing you. This book will show you new ways of seeing things, new ways of behaving and new actions that require time and practice to learn in order to grow and free yourself from habits and behaviors that no longer serve you. This book will equip you and your spirit to find the hope and strength for the climb by showing what it takes to keep faith, take heart and reach the top spiritually, emotionally, and financially intact.

This book can be a compass for the hard path through a necessary, perhaps even hostile divorce. It'll be well worth the read if you dare to have the courage to challenge these myths and heed the prudent principles. It may seem that your life is falling apart and you're rapidly in need of solid ground. You may inherently try to replace your falling ground with new beliefs that you now think will be true since you are divorcing. However, these too may be unsound. Once you begin to recognize these false beliefs, you can replace them with simple truths in action. These truths will guide you in the right direction through the pain and obstacles to rediscover yourself and navigate your way to an even brighter future. A future on solid ground, emotionally intact and still open to all that life has to offer.

My personal experience and common knowledge has shown that some paths have severe circumstances that warrant prudent caution and expert guidance. I am writing this book as a Professional Certified Life Coach and one who has climbed the hard path herself, not as a licensed therapist, lawyer or abuse counselor. Please, if you need these experts, go find them. I wouldn't want you to mistake the coaching I give in this book to stand in place of getting necessary support or police assistance. If you suspect or have already experienced such dire circumstances as violence, physical abuse and/or viable threats to loved ones, please for your safety and/or the safety of your children, I highly recommend privately seeking police protection and legal experts. Please trust yourself and your instincts first and foremost.

With that caution offered, I can tell you that you may be served by my personal experience, expertise and wisdom as a life coach. For you, I share two things:

The first is a set of Mean Time Myths: These are 12 core thoughts or beliefs that I noticed were most common in me and others on their path in the mean time. I list them one at a time; I then state a question for you to ask yourself; and finally I offer my 'coaching' insights on specific new thoughts and/or actions (antidotal) that can impact you and your path for the better.

The second is a set of Prudent Principles: These are important tidbits and savvy advice to keep in mind for prudence sake along your path. These are listed at the back of the book for ease of locating, so you can jump to and read them whenever you wish. They are to serve you in caring for yourself with sound information that will get you started on the right path and best supported for the climb.

Recognizing these myths and clearing them away by considering a new perspective and taking new actions helped me in the darkest of some very, very dark moments when knowing how to proceed was seemingly impossible. Unless your experts or attorney advises you otherwise, please use the Mean Time Myths and Prudent Principles to serve you and do your best to become a patient warrior.

Some of you reading this are now ready to get on with it and are eager to be fed. If you are one of them, feel free to jump ahead to the next section; however, I will caution you that you may have questions by doing so as the rest of this section will lay some ground work for reading the rest of the book. Others of you may be family and friends of the one going through this, if this is the case, I encourage you to continue with this section as it paints a wider picture for how your loved one got here and how you can be of service during this time of need.

Perhaps now in your divorce you are privately being threatened in a Dr. Jekyll - Mr. Hyde fashion to which you cannot possibly protect yourself adequately. Your other is making harmful threats when it's just you and no witnesses regarding what they believe or perceive that they can get away with. Your instinct may be to tell yourself that they're just losing it in this moment and as such immediately dismiss it from memory. This does not serve you. Threats such as having you or your children disappear or that as your spouse they have rights to your body and can take you sexually at any time they wish. Or perhaps you are finding that others you thought you could count on don't believe you and the extent of the psychological terror that is upon you, because you kept this dynamic private for too long. Instead of rallying behind you as you had hoped, they begin to question you and challenge your assessment of the situation. It becomes your word against the other.

Let me take a moment now to share with you why I will use the term the 'other' in this book. Most of us have heard the term 'ex' before and it has become the term used with negative connotation. I do not wish to inherit what comes with using that term. Also, regardless of what you believe your other may deserve, I find it will serve you most to begin neutralizing your emotions related to them. It can begin in language. How are you referring to them? Is it emotionally potent? The use of 'other' is a more neutral term. It simply states what is. This is the 'other' to you in this process.

Another way I intend to serve you in this book is by keeping my tone somewhat neutral. You will experience moments on your path that are filled with extremely strong emotions. I designed my verbiage in this book to attempt to comfort and calm you. My hope is that when you read just a bit of it, you will return to a state of neutrality, a more centered place for yourself. Chances are this will shift you to a better emotional state and you may find yourself able to breathe more easily. You may also gain access to new insights, thoughts or actions in this centered place that wouldn't have occurred to you in another strong emotional state. It can serve you and your body in navigating how best to proceed. That being said, in order to best give you the hindsight wisdom that is contained in this book, I was required to retrace my own mountain including the emotions that accompanied my climb. As such, you may notice that when I share certain past experiences, the emotional soup of that time may also carry onto the page. My intention is to dilute the soup somewhat, yet not completely, so as to fairly paint a picture of the mean time.

Regardless of how you feel about your other or what emotional state you are in, be advised. Your other may come up with ways of proceeding that you couldn't fathom, won't believe or even comprehend yourself. Your family or friends may get a call from your other. Chances are family members will decide to take it for better understanding on their part. While your other feigns upset and concern for you or your children to your friend, your other masterfully spins a false context which explains why they are calling, a real concern for you or the children, why you are not yourself and kindly asks them to see if they can talk some sense into you, since they themselves cannot. It's a brilliant maneuver that leaves your friend in complete confusion as is the intention, or worse your friend may even become your other's ally against you. Psychological warfare includes actively sabotaging your relationships with your family and friends to remove them from believing in and becoming a support to you. Take heart. Not everybody will buy it. There will be those in your corner. Your job is to find them and keep them close. Don't spend your energy on the rest. Any friends who do not want to take sides cannot be by your side through this.

Now that the other has created the impression that they are only acting out of true concern, compassion or protection for your own well-being, painting themselves as an angel, you are left to deal with the damage. You may be asking yourself, "How did I get here? How did I let this happen to me? How did I let myself get into a position where I'm powerless and my other has such leverage over me?" Please be gentle with yourself. Contrary to what you may be feeling, you didn't get here because you were stupid or a fool. You have a right to feel what you are feeling, but you didn't get here overnight.

First, you got here because slowly, over time you believed you were lovingly doing the right thing for everyone involved. You kept private what wasn't going right in your marriage and pressed on with patience in hope that someday your other would wake up and your marriage would change. You witnessed what appeared to be moments of awakening by your other, so you convinced yourself that it was just a matter of time before it would sustain.

Secondly, you discounted the times they would unmask this alternate persona and only remembered those times that matched your hopeful assessment of them. With time, you became adept at believing their words in spite of their behavior. You continued to give them the benefit of the doubt when they no longer deserved it. You may have even held on to a belief that you've been able to turn around other situations in the past and this too would eventually turn around as well, as long as you are patient, loving and keep giving it your all.

Third, by behaving and believing in such a way over time, when there was no evidence that true progress was being made, damage was created. The damage cannot be seen by others and you may not even recognize it yourself. Part of the damage is the separation of you from your family and friends by having kept this dynamic private. You seemingly protected them, your children and/or your other by not sharing about what was happening between you two. You didn't want to worry family or friends by sharing about what wasn't working in your marriage, believing it was just a matter of time before it would turn around. What you didn't count on was that when things eventually didn't turn around, you would have to catch them up quickly to the extent of what's been going on and how long you've been keeping them in the dark.

Last, you got here because things didn't go how you believed or knew they would. There is now a significant gap to how others now perceive your marriage and your firsthand experience of it. There will be no way to quickly catch others up to where you are now. You are in full crisis, but they are just learning that your relationship isn't what you led them to believe and what they thought it had been for sometime now. This gap will obstruct others from rapidly getting to where you will need them to be. You are in crisis and need them to quickly let go of their reality and get to yours now. You may be having appropriate levels of paranoia and terror about the extent of leverage that is in your other's control, including financial. You may be experiencing scary behavior in your other that those around you don't see. You may even continue to honor ridiculous requests by your other, hoping this will earn you better treatment and will alleviate their threats.

I write this next statement only with love... you need to wake up AND NOW! You need to accept now that the damage is done. Contrary to what you may be saying to yourself, you are not doing okay. You no longer need to attempt to placate your other and in fact you can't. If you keep on behaving in this way, it could get so much worse.

It's possible that you have lost a certain perspective of the reality of those around you by allowing yourself for too long to promote the pretense of how your marriage was going. You actively kept the unfortunate facts from others. Now, you are ready and need to move forward from your place of reference, but the others you need with you are greatly lagging behind. Maybe you truly believe that your friends and family will be on your side once you share with them what's been happening behind the scenes, or maybe you believe that if you hold on a little longer you will have earned some respectful 'quid pro quo'. Maybe you believe it's about the money, but haven't yet gleaned that it's about control. Money is just one way to control. Psychological warfare is another.

You too will have to rapidly shake off some false facts about the reality of how it's been going. You have lost perspective of the reality of those around you and as such you're assessing your path from what you believe will be true for them and for you, hence the myths. My intention in unveiling these Mean Time Myths and Prudent Principles for you is to gently guide you back to solid footing, so you can ground yourself in reality. You will need to compassionately engage and relate to those around you again, gently sharing with them the truth rather than your pretense which has become their reality. Be honest and responsible here. Make sure to apologize if need be. For protection and because at the time you believed it was the right thing to do, you led them to believe something false.

Let me first assure you that the situations I will refer to in this book are real and indeed happened. The persons will remain unnamed or renamed for protection sake and some examples may be a composite of true scenarios. Examples I share from my own experience are meant to serve others by sharing lessons learned from my own climb. I also share the examples in this book to demonstrate that no one is immune to this dynamic and that unknowingly any one of us can easily be victimized. My intention is for everyone to understand how these hidden manipulations occur and perpetuate. Together let's be aware and active in not causing harm or judgment to ourselves or to innocent others.

Ever hear the expression the best defense is a strong offense. Regardless of who may appear to be the victim, I will give you a hint for your own discernment. The one who is actively contacting others and goes public is most likely the perpetrator, even if they do so in tears. The true victim will not speak about it, NOT because they have something to hide as is the notion, but rather they've been forced to remain silent, as even more harm will come their way if it's discovered that they opened up about the true nature of their other. Chances are no one will believe the hidden truth vs. their own experience of that person anyway. The true victim will entrust the whole truth to very few.

My goal for you is to take heart and keep faith that you can create real, sustainable change for yourself and those around you; it's not just wishful thinking. By knowing the Mean Time Myths and Prudent Principles, you will have a better chance. This will take time. Remember you are in the mean time. I'm going to move you through these to help prepare you to have a healthier ground of reality so that you can get on beyond where you are now to a better place. Regardless of what happens in your outer circumstances, you'll be safeguarding your inner-core, so you don't come out of your divorce ground up, bitter, hostile, hating the other gender, or hating yourself and life. Rather you can come out with your self worth and dignity resurrected. Your ability to trust in yourself once again to create an even better future, to dream a new dream, one that this time can come true. Having faith that life will truly be joyous and fulfilling, even after the mean time.

HOW TO USE
THIS BOOK

My experience in coaching offers some insight in how you may read this book. You may believe that if you just try harder, see things a certain way or wait around a little bit longer, things will change, so you may read this book, yet not attempt its guidance. Or you may use the guidance of one myth and if it works, conclude that the rest will work or visa versa. Or you may begin to use these myths as a comparison, to measure your progress or perhaps beat yourself up if you didn't recognize them yourself. Please be gentle with yourself and try not to use this book in this matter. Rather it is meant to be used as a compass, a handy tool to guide you in navigating your own way. The mean time myths offer great insight and guidance, but above all else, they will require your input too. All myths are not meant to fit everyone, yet some will fit most. You must use your own discernment for the ones that fit. Trust and believe in yourself and your instincts. Only you know your situation with your other. I do not.

If you're wondering about how I understand and know how you can get lost or stuck in the mean time, let me give you my story in brief. Wahl Smiley and I started out on equal footing at the beginning of our marriage. We were both in our mid-twenties, both college graduates, and successful professionals in our respective fields. I was an engineer and he was in finance. We each made a good living, about the same in annual income, with no liabilities such as debt or student loans. Everything we built, we built together in our marriage. All assets, liquidity, and personal property were marital, unless inherited or gifted. We both supported the idea of having the choice over whether or not I would exit the workforce when we had children. When that time came, with Wahl's verbal support, I did.

I reinvented myself when I became a mother. The most important factor I learned about being a good mother is finding the path of something that gives you purpose and makes you happy. My mother was a career woman and worked full-time throughout my childhood. My step-mother and grand-mothers did not. I have a loving and incredible relationship with each of them. I experienced first hand that neither path is right nor wrong, both have value. I loved being an engi-neer, and when my children came along, I found purpose and wanted to be with my children more. Now that my children are somewhat grown, I love and have found an expanded purpose in being a life coach and working full-time once again. This book is for all women, mothers or not, working at a job or working at home.

In my case, leaving the field of engineering and relying on my husband's income took an incredible leap of faith. I relied on myself to support me financially, so much so that I earned a full academic scholarship to put me through college. However, in my heart I felt it was a risk worth taking. Since my commitment is to keep this book short and simple, I will pass on spelling out the sad demise of our marriage other than to say this... From my perspective, after years of being brutally honest with him about how I felt in how our marriage and what wasn't working, sometimes in tears and other times by yelling at him about what needed to change. I patiently gave him four years to seek marriage counseling together and save our marriage, only to be consistently met with "no". After too much time, I was no longer willing or able to be discounted. I was no longer willing to be neglected and emotionally manipulated and abused. Over years, he dismissed and disrespected me as a woman, wife and mother in front of our children and my family. The way I see it now, he saw me as his property, a trophy to display. Once he won it, he no longer needed to tend to it. My inner core, my soul and my heart were no longer cared for, no longer his concern. He was happy. He got everything he wanted. I was the one who was upset. I was the one who wasn't happy; therefore, I was the one who must be the issue in the relationship. He would use my background and past to sell me a perspective on how it's my fault that I'm unhappy, that I need too much, etc... He would bring up my personal stories, vulnerabilities, and insecurities to rationally use them against me as to why I was unhappy, something he had nothing to do with. When all along, I simply needed love, something he did not have to give. The outwards of our relationship looked good; the inwards of our relationship were rotting. It might easily appear to others now like the story of the chicken and the egg... which came first? Did I leave him because of how he treated me? Or does he treat me this way because I left him? I was there at the beginning. I walked each day of this relationship with patience and love. No matter how much I loved and honored him and how much I gave to make it work, it didn't and couldn't make the difference that only he was responsible to make, to love and honor in return. He chose not to and by doing so ended our relatedness and ultimately our marriage. That's the sad truth.

Why then would I think the divorce would be any different?

Despite his assurance of amicability in the divorce, Wahl illegally cut me off from my portion of marital assets all while having a steady income of about $25,000/month. He then used our marital assets against me. He began spending them by suing me for sole custody of our children, all marital property and assets, and even his legal expenses. At the time, I had a minimal income as a life coach due to being the primary caregiver of our children and had been out of the workforce as an engineer for over 10 years. By setting up a new business account and by placing passcodes on our joint accounts as the primary account holder, Wahl had now arranged it so that within minutes I had no access to my legal portion of martial income or assets. Conversely, he was financially potent with both his six-figure income and his autonomous access to both portions of marital assets. Once he pulled the trigger, he mistakenly strategized and believed that I would have no means to get to Court and would be forced to settle the divorce on his terms alone.

Perhaps it is that most epic stories are trilogies, as our epic divorce had three stages: seemingly amicable —» increasingly difficult —» combative divorce. Stage one was discussing our divorce in private with one another alone. Wahl and I seemingly agreed to privately discuss and agree to what we each believed to be the best outcome for all involved before contacting attorneys and telling our families and friends. Later, it was proven that I was the only one to honor that agreement, which ultimately set a web for me to be ensnared. We spent months, separated in the same household, privately discussing our divorce and how it would go. Yes, months! During that time, it was agreed that he would keep the house and I would move into a smaller residence that I could afford with the spousal and child support I would receive, until I could build back my own income. This seemingly amicable stage ended up taking 10 months, instead of what was supposed to be weeks, due to Wahl convincing me to go slow due to his fears about what his family would think, etc…, but was later revealed to be a concealed strategy on his part.

Stage two of our divorce was in the collaborative divorce process and painstakingly took the next 11 months, four experts (two attorneys and two clinical psychologists), we even brought in a retired Judge with great credibility, experience and noble spirit to try and resolve our differences. All the while I was financially responsible for my portion of this process, as he continued to be unwilling to provide me access to my portion of marital funds. The collaborative divorce process required paying all of these professionals their fee which amounted in excess of tens of thousands of dollars with even worse results, requiring that process to be cancelled and begin again from scratch for stage three. This final stage was the litigation divorce process which I now strongly believe to be the only prudent process to finalize any divorce when dealing with a highly combative and controlling spouse. It took another 9 months and approximately $100,000 dollars just for my legal representation alone to finally achieve the divorce decree.

As in our marriage, Wahl did not honor who I was or respect me and my abilities in our divorce. He didn't count on my faith and perseverance. He used my amicability against me and once that came to light felt that I would be so betrayed that I wouldn't have the strength to stand up to him. He couldn't know I would find and sustain other substantive financial means, thanks to what my mother had set aside for my inheritance. I was able to use the law to fight for my legal and parental rights. He didn't know I had the mental toughness required to stay and fight fairly every inch of the way no matter how long it took. He underestimated my resolve, my ability and my skill to become what would be required of me as a loving mother, a noble warrior, and a healing soul.

After navigating my path, climbing my mountain and reaching the top, when my divorce settlement was final after legally being married for 12 years, I received what I believed to be an equitable portion of what was left of all marital assets, personal property, spousal and child support. Although I needed my mother's financial support to divorce, I am now able to provide for my family without my husband's or anyone else's financial support. Instead of being paid alimony, I agreed to receive an upfront lump sum settlement payment for that purpose. Tax laws are such that property settlements are non-taxable, whereas alimony would've been taxable income. Something you may wish to keep in mind. I received a settlement payment of half of the equity in our marital home. I own and reside in a beautiful townhome with my loving husband and children. We have a love and respect for one another in a loving marriage that I couldn't have dreamt possible. My husband and I enjoy being a blended family and share joint custody of the children with Wahl. I continue to receive child support, which is less than 10% of Wahl's monthly income, but sufficient for additional support of the children. He also paid to me the equivalent to what he paid his own attorney which I contributed to my legal fees. We split equitably what was left of the retirement and investment portfolios. I both healed and fought with dignity for my legal rights, for what I believed was in the highest and best interest for everyone involved and I didn't walk away from anything that I wasn't okay with leaving. To be honest it wasn't what I had hoped for, but I could live with it. My freedom and health and the freedom and health of our children were by far the best settlement I made.

From where I stand today, much of my climb could have been made easier or cut shorter. My ability to accept new realities and move on more quickly would have been possible if I had such a book to read and guide me, to unveil these mean time myths and the coaching antidotes that would help me to keep faith, take heart and continue to climb. I name these myths the Mean Time Myths for two reasons. The first is somewhat obvious that you are in between the life that is falling away and the life that you have yet to create, so you are in the meantime. Also your other may become surprisingly cruel and unpredictable, so I'm using in the mean time because it can become rather mean.

The following examination of the Mean Time Myths and the coaching I offer here are meant to serve, challenge, expand and support you by grounding yourself in reality. They are not meant to replace your own personal experiences, beliefs or thoughts. These myths were unveiled, noticed and captured by me as an experienced certified life coach as I and others shared about our mean time journeys. The coaching I offer is what I learned and acquired myself. My intention in my climb was to do whatever it took to rightfully honor what was in the highest and best interest for all involved. I both fought with dignity and healed at the same time. Most in similar un-amicable situations don't have the guidance on how to do both. They falsely believe that they only have the strength to do one or the other. That is, they believe they only have strength to fight hard for what is needed to rebuild, but end up bitter. Or they believe they only have strength to heal, so end up giving in, but are not equipped to rebuild. Doing what you can to do both at the same time is a better path and can be done. It honors your part in the marriage and what you built together. It honors your self worth and dignity. It honors your legal and parental rights and provides better means to build a new future. It's the best way for you to remain wholly intact.

I trust that you will be served by reading all of the

Mean Time Myths, including the questions to ask yourself and the coaching; however, only you will be responsible and have choice over which of these to follow. Some of them may fit, others may not. I do not presume to know your specific situation nor whether it is in your best interest to use the coaching as notated in these myths. I do however know these myths are common and that the coaching can serve when there is a match. Please take full responsibility for doing what you believe to be right. Listen to your experts and heed their advice. These are being offered here in conjunction to help you chart your own course, one that will be worth it to you.

My main goal in sharing these myths is to hopefully remind you of who you still are, why you came, where you are and what you can look forward to. On an airplane when turbulence hits and there's a loss of oxygen, an air mask is needed. Only now the turbulence is your life and there's a loss of certainty, support and how best to proceed, you need a compass. These mean time myths are a way to ground yourself in the reality of your situation by giving you core wisdom, some practical guidance, emotional support, and companionship when you feel alone. This book will show you that you are not alone and can lift your spirits and guide you back to yourself and to what's possible by serving you to chart your own personalized path and reach the top of your mountain. Good luck and keep climbing!

MYTH ONE

*"If I just give them what they're asking for,
this will all go away and end."*

QUESTION: Is it going away? Is it ending?

COACHING: You may be in denial. You may be torn between what you believe is possible vs. what is actually happening. Widen your gaze. Pay attention to your other's actions and inactions. What have they done or are doing? What have they not done or are not doing? Are they attempting to redeem themselves and soothe you by promising you something else out into the future? See them for who they are. They do not have your interest at heart. Do not look to their words, promises, demeanor or charm as they are clever at using these gifts to delude you and others. They continually appear authentic as though they truly mean and believe in what they are saying. Do they however fail to deliver on their promises and instead perpetually come up with justified reasons or excuses? This cycle is a way to control and dominate you and will continue endlessly if you allow it. The only choice you have to stop it is to be strong enough to say no more. Draw a line in the sand, the line of demarcation, this far no further. There is no other way for the cycle to stop. You must be strong! Only you can end it.

On my path, I gave Wahl what he asked for in return for his solemn promise to remain amicable through out our divorce. After declaring our marriage was over and immediately separating bedrooms, I assured him that I would remain amicable. He then assured amicability if I would move back to the other coast, back to where we had lived the previous years. I considered what was in everyone's best interest, and I made the move back, taking the risk to leave a 'no fault' state by doing so. I believed in my heart that an amicable divorce would be best for everyone so I agreed to return, since I believed him in his promise of amicability. Sadly, a promise he never kept.

Please be aware. They use open communication as a means to spy on you and gather ammunition. This may be your natural habit. You may also believe that open communication supports an amicable process. I'd rather you consider that it can also be a way for them to create confidentiality with you, to keep tabs on you, to get information and inappropriate agreements from you. It will also be a way for them to impact your energy. They can soothe and calm you by making believable promises. Or they can deplete you by remaining in an irrational diatribe. Any conversations with them that you willingly kept private can later be denied that they ever took place. It'll be your word against theirs. You will have no one to back you up on this, because you were honorable, and kept the agreed upon confidences. As such, it will be in your best interest from now on to have all conversations documented, in written form. This means email only. I highly encourage you to get guidance before you respond, especially to anything that causes a reaction in you where you feel the need to respond immediately. Please remember urgency is usually a servant of darkness, not the Light. You will learn that not everything will need a response. It will be wise to consult with your attorney, find one who is a noble soul and has mastery in negotiating.

Yes. This means no longer speak to the other via phone or in person without your attorney present. Consider you believe that you are alleviating their concerns and are making progress by staying in open communication with them, and that if you cut them off, things will get worse. Whether or not this is the case, I guarantee you things will definitely get worse if you continue to do the same thing that you've been doing, expecting a different result. Please listen and learn from my own miss-steps here.

An example of how my amicability didn't serve me on my own path was when I remained in open communication and created amicable agreements with my other, until it became abundantly clear that my other was being covert about his true nature and un-amicable intentions. Please give me some time to paint this picture fully now here in myth #1 for all the other myths as well.

It began when we moved back. Wahl had tricked me into keeping my distance and friendship with new neighbors, saying he didn't want to look like "the bad guy" once our divorce became public. Since we had already privately agreed that he would be the one staying in the house, he didn't want these new neighbors to get close to me. He shared his concern that they might think of him later as "the asshole who kicked me out", so he asked me not to make friends or get close with them. For the benefit of our children's future with their neighborhood friends and classmates and to maintain mutual respect for both parents in the neighborhood, I mistakenly honored his request and never shared the details of our situation with these neighbors.

After months of keeping our divorce private from them, once I moved out for my own safety, Wahl took full advantage. He had pre-set the stage so that these new neighbors knew little about me and nothing about us and our ongoing divorce. He understood that our divorcing would no longer be private. These new neighbors probably saw the van in the driveway when for my own protection, my mom secretly helped move me and my personal belongings out of the house while he was out of town for the weekend. Instead of saying that we had been privately divorcing, residing on separate levels and in separate bedrooms of the house for over 1 year now, since before moving back to the state. He neglected to mention that I had filed a report with the county crisis center against him due to his behavior and actions. He didn't say that even with my family's financial support to fund a separate residence for me, he still wouldn't agree for me to move out and begin the 1 year count-down for legal separation. He never mentioned that he had violated our collaborative divorce process by secretly being in communication with a litigating attorney; the same litigating attorney who later represented him when he filed suit against me in Court. He failed to mention that due to his hidden guise, the situation at home and his behavior had become so dire that both clinical psychologists in our collaborative divorce encouraged me to move out that very weekend. Unlike his violation, these experts had full knowledge and even encouraged mine; as they also deemed it necessary for my own safety. They began to see the situation more clearly now as he still wouldn't agree for me to leave when there was no rational reason why he shouldn't. His reason was hidden.

He had to stall in order to reset status quo. He wasn't ready to begin the count-down, so he couldn't agree to let me leave and legally separate. He knew I couldn't leave without his agreement or else he would bring suit against me for abandonment. He was misusing this collaborative process until he had the 1 year under his belt of his new parenting structure, showing times working from home, no more travel and now participating in the children's extracurricular activities as head coach and all doctor's visits, something he was never able to do in our marriage despite my multiple requests to have that kind of schedule during the first 8 years of our marriage. He would say all the right things to these experts by simply feigning fearfulness about going public with the divorce. Voila! He continually used my belief in his amicability to set me up and used it all against me later. Ten months after separating bedrooms and moving back, we began the collaborative divorce process, an amicable process requiring full disclosure. I didn't understand yet that this was only to give him the necessary time to set the stage in his favor before suing me in Court. Believing in his amiability, I disclosed that I had begun dating someone else as is required to disclose everything in the collaborative divorce process. Repulsively, Wahl then offered to bed me stating that "it would legally take adultery off the table" for me. Could it be that his intent was to take it off the table for himself? When I refused his advances, in an instant he showed his true nature and the great plan that he and his litigating attorney had been creating all along. Legally, psychologically, emotionally, and financially take me out fully and I would no longer have the resources to fight. Then if I still wanted a divorce, it would be under his terms alone. The added bonus of his misuse of the collaborative divorce process was publicly making me 'persona non grata' by naming me an adulterer to our new neighbors and various others.

Mr. Smiley told these neighbors that he kicked me out of the house and is now filing for divorce claiming that he had found me with this other man. These neighbors did not know that he was calculatedly misleading them by excluding certain facts and spinning others out of context simply to ruin my credibility and gain their favor. He knew that if he painted it this way, it would ruin my credibility with them and they would no longer speak openly to me. Thus, they would only have his version of events, absent from mine. Once this falsehood was seeded, it could not be undone, especially without me speaking the whole truth. He used their own experiences of seeing us together as a seemingly happily married couple, under false pretense, to back up what he was saying. He already had all the leverage over me that I wasn't going to provoke him further by outing his misrepresentation to his neighbors. It was nothing short of malicious. I had no choice but to let it lie! Besides what would I say? Who would I believe if I were them? And if they believed me, chances are these neighbors would simply back away from us altogether and consequently our children to avoid added conflict. As always, I thought of our children and didn't want it to impact their ability to keep their friends in that neighborhood. For their sake, I remained silent.

Consider the possibility that your other sees you as the opposition, as a threat. Even if you aren't, they won't see it any other way. Whether you believe it or not, you need to be aware now that you are speaking into enemy camp. At least believe they do not have your best interest at heart. They can become wickedly clever and may be using your kindness and amicability to collect information, your confidentiality or to set a stage to use against you later. They are not your advocate. Now that you are divorcing, there is no reason to give them the courtesy of being in open or confidential communication with them!

I understand that this may be very upsetting to hear, but I'm intentionally exposing it for what it is. Be very clear. I'm your friend and advocate. I'm not against them as it may sound. Rather, I'm for protecting yourself and maintaining a level playing field. Contrary to how you may feel, this is not being rude to them. By their own behavior, they no longer have rights to your courtesy and kindness! You must stop giving it! From now on, if you must speak to them only do so when your attorney is present. When they attempt to coerce you into a diatribe by saying things like, you're the one not cooperating, please just speak to me it's something simple, we don't need to pay our attorneys for, etc... remain calm, don't respond to their words or questions. Instead, kindly ask them to send you an email with whatever they wish to discuss and that you'll take a look at it.

*"You forged my love just like a weapon,
and you turned it against me like a knife. You broke
my last heart-string, you opened up my eyes."*

*"Growing up is not the absence of dreaming;
it's being able to understand the difference between the ones
you can hold and the ones that you've been sold."*

—LYRICS BY JEWEL

(from *Goodbye Alice in Wonderland*)

MYTH**TWO**

"I'm becoming like the other."
(confrontational, stubborn, unreasonable, etc...)

QUESTION: Do you find yourself recognizing behavior, emotions and parts of conversations in yourself that you once saw disapprovingly in the other?

COACHING: Be careful with yourself. In other words, be full of care with yourself. You are growing and expanding into a new territory of learning with the other: how to effectively say no and stand up for yourself.

When you find yourself unable to discern if what's being offered or asked of you is fair or equivalent, here's my suggestion. Regarding what is being asked of you, if all factors were in the reverse, would you ask (or offer) the same of them (to them)? If no, chances are it's not a fair or equivalent offer or request. Say so and stand your ground for something else that is.

Please recognize that you are not becoming like the other, you are simply gaining strength in the necessary skill of saying no by effectively arguing your case and standing your ground with them. This may be new to you. If so, I can promise you you're going to be rather poor at it before you get good at it. However, remind yourself each day that you are getting better. Remember you are coming from fairness, which includes caring for yourself too now. What internally motivates you to say no and stand your ground is up to you. That's all you need to know.

On my path, standing up for myself required canceling the collaborative divorce process which was very costly and painful, but crucial as nothing would move forward without Wahl's agreement, so the only agreements ever made during that process were in his favor alone. I was only losing money and even more ground in this wasted process. There was no collaboration and these experts held no authority over him.

Please be patient. You may initially find yourself incapable of saying no, making your case and effectively standing your ground with them, especially if they hold the cards to your freedom. Give yourself as much time to learn these new and much needed behaviors as you gave the other to change. This will take time. Anything less is simply impatience on your part.

"One of the most aggressive things a human being can do is to go against what he or she believes is nice or pretty... changes ONLY happen when we go totally against everything we're used to doing... only one thing will remain in tact—your children. They are the connecting thread, and you must respect that."

—PAULO COELHO

(from *The Witch of Portobello*)

MYTH THREE

"I'd rather forgive and forget." Literally!

QUESTION: Ever hear the expression, "Those who forget the past are destined to repeat it?"

COACHING: No one other than you was there and has the information necessary to depict an accurate view of all that has transpired, all that has been perpetrated, and even all that has been forgiven.

*If you don't remember, if you don't speak up, no one else will!

You may feel heavy, weighted down and drained by remembering or discussing these unpleasant facts. You may feel it even more now due to the fact that it may be getting worse and seemingly endless. Perhaps your way of dealing with this drain was to simply forgive and forget about them. Although forgiving most likely helped you, forgetting has not and will not serve you now or in the future. There are other ways to deal with the heaviness rather than forgetting.

In my experience, what I'm asking next will be rather hard for you to do, but it will be necessary for you if you wish to level the playing field for fairness. Consider the other is a natural at keeping score; you are not. As such, they are prevailing in remembering and reframing facts easily in the moment to their advantage, an essential tool in negotiations. Naturally you don't keep score, so you will lose ground here unless you commit to grow this skill. It can be done. It will take time.

To begin, keep a journal with you at all times, perhaps in your purse or car. Write down important facts as you remember them. Throughout your day, certain memories or important events will naturally come to mind, perhaps triggered by an external source. When you remember them, capture them in your journal as soon as you can. This is your natural way of remembering, not under fire. Use your journal as a storehouse for your memories. You can then refer to your memories before your meetings. Bring it with you to your meetings. It will serve as your memory when you're under fire. Feel free to ask for time to refer to it when you need to.

Also, starting now, journal daily about what is currently transpiring, only the important facts, not everything. Are there any current violations of agreements, tardiness, threats or absurd comments? Keep track of them starting today. As soon as possible, record in as much detail what transpired, including dates and times. There will rarely be a witness for these occasions, but if so, make a note. Even if it was as simple as a neighbor coming out of their house to collect their mail, make a note of it. By capturing these simple and trivial details, the more you are believed that it actually took place and you captured it at that moment. Once you've recorded the incident, you can let it go, but capture it as best as you can before you forget.

As you begin, chances are you won't want to do it or remember to do it. For your own care, you must. Again, no one other than you was there and has the information necessary to depict a grounded view of all that has transpired, all that has been perpetrated and all that has been forgiven.

Word of Caution: As tempted as you may be at times when the other is misbehaving to use these tidbits against them, please control yourself. This tool is for you alone to grow your skill at remembering. The information you capture will have it's time and place, you and your attorney together will decide what to reveal. You may also feel like your throwing the other under the bus when that time comes. So be it. You are simply standing up for yourself with detailed facts. You did not start this. Consider an equal measured response of your data in conflict of theirs is playing fairly. You are simply leveling the playing field by enhancing your memory and countering their skill in equal measure. Nothing more.

"All the world is full of suffering.
It is also full of overcoming."

~ HELEN KELLER

MYTH**FOUR**

"It's too much. It's too hard. It's too heavy to bear."

QUESTION: Compared to what?

COACHING: Sometimes the path of the warrior is simply staying on the path. There will be times when you feel invincible. There will be other times when you are certain that you're greatest fear is coming to fruition. There will be no way to see beyond the next step. You will have no idea where this mountain is taking you. In fact, at times you'll be in such misery and despair that you'll begin looking for a way off the mountain. The only way off that you will find is even more miserable than what you are dealing with in the moment. It's usually giving up or giving in to your greatest fear come true.

Let me take a moment to share with you what may be perceived as darkness. There are three layers of how it may be perceived. Layer one (1) is the weight and heaviness or drain of energy that happens when you engage in activities or conversations. Some of these will be a must and will serve you to effectively complete your path, such as attending meetings with your other or naming the unpleasant behaviors or threats that you've been receiving. This will be extremely uncomfortable, but necessary for experts to be in the know. Layer two (2) is at the behavioral level and something that you may need to rebuild. Chances are that you've been behaving defensively for so long that you see taking the offense as aggressive, an attack or dark. You will need to let go of your interpretation that this behavior is in anyway dark and step into it. You will need to in order to create balance and a level playing field. You must grow your offense. Lastly layer three (3) of darkness are the unseen forces that tempt you to surrender, take urgent action or make inappropriate decisions, actions or agreements.

WORD OF CAUTION: This layer of darkness will tempt you to become impatient. It will use your thoughts to forecast into the future. It will appear that you are running out of resources and energy for that future that's to come. The attempt is to entice you to no longer have the strength to carry on, luring you to go ahead and simply surrender now. Avoid prolonging the misery and just get it over with. Now! NEVER LISTEN TO THIS DARKNESS! You may not be able to quiet these thoughts, but do not act on them! EVER! Even though they seem very real, they are merely thoughts. Ask yourself if you have enough resources and energy for the present timeframe. Do not look into the future, as new opportunities may arise between now and then. This is your fear talking: false evidence appearing real. You will need to be strong. It too will pass.

I will give you the metaphor that helped me when darkness came to my path. I would think of a car with headlights driving through the darkness. The headlights can only light the way directly in front of the car, but not further down the road. It therefore makes sense to only drive forward as far as the headlights can show and not worry about what lies ahead. If you look beyond the lit path only darkness will be seen. Stay focused on what's directly in front of you, still in the light. Just like driving, it won't serve you to try to see beyond what's lit. As you already know, it doesn't mean that darkness will still reside there when you arrive to that part of the path. By the time you reach that part, the headlights will still be with you and can shine the way forward from there, but not from here. Don't expect your headlights to shine all the way down your path from here that would be absurd. We live in time and space. Many things can alter the path ahead between now and when you arrive to that future place. Just keep focused on what's already lit for you to travel and move steadily forward along your path.

The woods are dense, and filled with doubts and fears.
Yet, there is a light at the edge,
which through the darkness sears.
The path is shown,
but step by step-
that way alone.
Patiently follow it,
rush not ahead.
There are many pits,
truly harmless
if the light is used,
to guides one's progress;
crippling or deadly to one,
who finds that she
must jump the gun.
Hard and hazardous is the way.
Except when the light
through the woods conveys.

—JAMES S. WINNER

MYTHFIVE

"If you don't have something nice to say,
don't say anything at all."

QUESTION: Are you speaking positively about yourself? To yourself? How about to others?

COACHING: Rather than remain silent, speak about it. Do this in balance. You must get it out, but only to a few. Those you can trust are on your side alone. You can start to do this powerfully by becoming your own personal advocate. Share in appropriate settings some of the more painful facts and how you did the fair thing even in the mean time. Share the joyous ones too: stories of you as a friend, as a sister, as mom, as a daughter or neighbor, etc.... Most of us are unaware that our storytelling and the stories we tell give others accurate glimpses of who we really are in both the good times and the bad. Everyone will get to know you even more this way, not just by spending time with you.

Do you feel like you're getting a glimpse of who I am by reading this book?

Here's a story from my own experience. Awhile after separating households yet before the divorce decree was signed and after much consideration, I shared with my children that I was dating my now husband. They asked me if this meant that the divorce was now final. Here's what I shared with them...

You both just completed the school year, right? Yet you haven't received your report cards in the mail yet have you? Does this mean you didn't complete your grade? Does it mean that you didn't do everything there was for you to do? No. It simply means that you're waiting on others to get you your report card. It's the same with divorce. Some people believe that it's not final until they receive the document, like the report card. Others believe that it's final when you've done all there was for you to do, and you are now waiting for what needs to be done by others to complete the document and get it to you. It depends on how you see it.

MYTHSIX

"How did I get here? How can I have been so stupid?
Am I losing my mind?"

QUESTION: Are you pondering whether or not it is you or someone else who has lost their marbles?

COACHING: You are completely fine. You are simply caught in the mean time. Be on the lookout. Be patient and diligent. The other may try and trap you with your own emotional reactions to their distorted facts about your mutual reality. Some will attempt to provoke you with absurd and inaccurate comments, hoping to make you appear emotionally unstable, retaliatory even, when you refute them. Try to remain calm as best as you can. Recognize that your own emotions and behavior may work against you. Similar to a neglected and emotionally abused animal, the outward behavior is the result of the perpetrations and abuses inflicted upon them. This reaction is not of their choosing. This is a habitual response to how they've been treated over time.

In the presence of your other, consider you have been trained over time to shut down when it may serve you to speak up and to speak up or react when it may serve you to remain silent. As such, the same behavior in you may occur in any conversations when the other is present. You may appear overly reactive when you should be calm or visa versa. Your reactions may appear out of proportion to what is considered to be the norm, making it appear like you are the unstable one. This dynamic can be used against you by the other. They will say or do things to provoke you so that you are the one who looks like you're not grounded in reality, not them. Do not take the bait! Remember the experts, neighbors, friends or family do not have the larger context that only you have: the years of neglect and emotional harassment. Furthermore, in meetings with the experts, the other has the capacity to trick themselves in believing their own falsehood in order to manipulate their behavior to be congruent with what they are claiming. By doing so, the other can manipulate the experts, friends, neighbors, and family in believing what he is saying is true. What you see is

NOT what you get. So much so, that I believe the other may even be able to pass a polygraph.

Never doubt your truth or your belief in yourself! You know the truth. However, to the others, you both will look like you're telling the truth; they will not share your discernment for which one is lying. Try your best to listen from what these others who do not know the truth are hearing. As difficult as it is and as in the twilight zone as you feel, please try your best to calm yourself and your energy. Do your best to respond and not to react. Use specific detailed facts from the offensive, not the defensive. Take the time to paint the picture in full for those who weren't there. Do not allow the other to interrupt you when you are doing so. Do not answer the other's questions directed at you, they use this tactic to confuse you and get you off point. Instead respond by ignoring them altogether or come up with a counter question to ask them that furthers your point. You will be best heard if you are not in the reaction of disbelief, shock, disgust, anger, frustration, etc... Try. Please try to be calm. It will take time to expose the full context of what the other is up to that others won't see or even believe immediately. Remain steady as best as you can. With time and practice you will get there. Only with time, others will have the chance to see it if you remain calm and courageous enough to continually point it out to them. The other will eventually betray themselves with their own words. They will attempt to launch malicious insults intended to cause you harm, but instead reveal just how irrational they can be. One such example of this was when I announced moving in with my now husband while he was still my fiancé. After contacting our Custody Evaluator to get her input on how to proceed for the best care for the children, she said simply that she didn't even know why I would need to check in with her. I replied simply that it wasn't because of a concern of mine, but rather for how Wahl would react when he was told. She said simply that if he has any issue with it, to have him give her a call. At a following meeting with our Parent Coordinator, with her support, I told him. The response by my other was intense. He verbally threatened me in front of her. He said, "If you do, I will sue you for sodomy!" After seeing the doctor's and my reaction of shock, he continued by stating, "You know, when two people live together and are not married." Our Parent Coordinator asked that I leave the meeting, so she could finish with him alone. She later emailed me that the meeting ended well and felt that she made a real difference with him. An assessment that I knew only time would reveal to be valid or not. Time showed her what I already had experienced firsthand and thus did foresee, that as much as she felt that conversation had made a 'real' difference, given her perception of his response and the agreements for what he would do following that meeting. These were never delivered upon. No real difference could ever be made without him genuinely taking responsibility for his own part in the demise of our marriage.

Use these moments to shine your light for all to see, as you already do, how absurdly irrational and distorted they and their threats can be. You are simply moving forward into a new life with prudence, taking action and freeing yourself regardless of what your other will do or think.

"Success is not final. Failure is not fatal.
It's the courage to continue that counts."

—WINSTON CHURCHILL

MYTH SEVEN

"The other is better at this than you are."

QUESTION: Who wants what's in the best interest for everyone involved most?

COACHING: You are already equipped with all you need. Consider this is the case, because you have been at the receiving end of the other for as long as you have. You actually know what to do. You know how to do it. You just don't want to do it.

*You haven't realized yet that you have no choice but to fight for what's your right if you truly want it to be fair. As much as you're not a fighter, you must engage in this fight in equal measure. Your choice to not fight has not kept the other from doing so. Yes, it wasn't started by you, but only you can make it a level playing field by fighting back. Not to do so will result in you bringing the unfairness to the fight, not the other way around. Only with your full engagement will there be a chance for a level playing field, fairness and the highest and best interests for all to be heard.

On my path, Mr. Smiley persuaded the experts that he was as equally active in the children's lives these previous years giving the example that he was the one who got up with the children in the morning and I was the one who put them to bed at night. What he left out was that him getting up with them in the morning was spending the ~15 minutes that it took to get them out of their rooms and place them in front of the TV to watch cartoons or play video games. I would then get up around 7 am and was the one who took care of the next 12 hours plus solo. I am the one who provided for them the rest of their day until they went to sleep that night around 7:30 pm, which included not only the full morning routine, but the afternoon and bedtime routine solo as well. Just the morning routine included getting them changed, brushed, dressed, preparing breakfast, feeding them and cleaning up afterwards, this all occurred after he had left for work. Wahl however led them to assume that getting up with them meant he did the full morning routine with them instead of me. Make it fair by speaking up. Give yourself time. It took me awhile to build back my ability to respond with calmness and in equal measure. I eventually leveled any deceitfulness using my demeanor, assertiveness and the detailed facts.

"God does not call the equipped.
He equips the called."

MYTH**EIGHT**

"People closest to you will support you.
They will understand what you're going through and
will be there for you through thick and thin."

QUESTION: How much did you share with them when things were going downhill?

COACHING: If they want to stay connected to both of you or if they want to stay neutral with your children, they will not be an advocate either way. Be fair to yourself (and to them), which may mean make new friends, ones that will be your advocate alone. Be patient. This will take time.

When movers were coming to move my piano and office furniture out of the marital home, I had made arrangements with someone I considered to be a dear friend for over 4 years to come and meet us at the house. I needed a neutral witness to see that the items being removed from the marital home were agreed upon by both parties and also so as not to be alone with Wahl. That morning about 15 minutes before she was to meet me, she phoned me on my cell. I was already parked in the neighborhood waiting for the movers to arrive. She told me that she was unable to make it. In an instant I thought she was joking, so I laughed and said, "Ha ha, very funny!" She paused and then replied, "No really, I'm not coming."

I fell silent. I couldn't believe my ears. Heartbroken, I was shocked. Did she not understand what this meant? Did she not understand how much I needed her? That having someone else with me was imperative? Why did she wait until the last minute to tell me? Why couldn't she have called me sooner, so I had time to find someone else? After she hung up, I quickly went to one of the neighbors and asked if she could help me. She didn't hesitate. This generous act of kindness made her an instant hero for me in a great time of need.

Unavoidable heartbreak may reside here. Friends and family you thought you could trust may betray you or your trust. They may do so unknowingly by giving information to the other that you've been keeping to protect yourself or your children. These friends and family think they are being helpful by keeping the peace. They have no idea of the potential harm they are causing by remaining in communication with the other.

Not comprehending the full extent of Wahl's irrational behavior and threats, my mother privately accepted a phone call from him, during which he attempted to turn her against me. During that call, she informed him that she would be a support to me and that in fact she was moving me out of the house that weekend. She didn't tell me this until later. As you can imagine, this was very upsetting for me to hear. I understood that she had the best of intentions, but this was not helpful for her to do. However, God winked, as it was in this very conversation she experienced first hand what I had been trying to tell her about Wahl that she couldn't yet comprehend or even believe herself. They only slip under intense pressure. This news gave it to him. She finally experienced what I had been trying to convey to her and only now fully comprehended.

Great joy may also reside here. There will be "hidden heroes." People you never knew had your back. They will come out of nowhere. They will be incredible, empathetic listeners. They will donate lifesaving time and resources to you when you need them most. Experience is a trade they will have. This is part of the joy you will experience on this journey. Delight in their generosity and love!

Thank goodness at the very beginning I had the intelligence to immediately disclose all that was transpiring with Wahl and our divorce to one of my dear friends. I knew I could trust her to keep it private. I shared fully about all of it, including his request to move back to assure amicability.

In the litigation process, Wahl was denying that we had declared our marriage over at that time and all the rest since; I needed a witness that could testify firsthand to these true facts. She willingly and courageously stepped forward. She had been to my home, knew that we were in separate bedrooms, and still had the calendar with her handwritten notes on the day that we met and discussed it all even. Moreover, she knew our entire family's history and had firsthand experience with each of us over the years of our marriage. She knew the whole truth and became my star witness, which required her to be ready to make a last minute flight all the way to the opposite coast, including having the care of her children handled by others while she was gone. Words are simply insufficient to capture the extent of the hero she was for me in my greatest hour of need.

"That's what it takes to be a hero, a little gem
of innocence inside you that makes you want to believe
that there still exists a right and wrong, that decency
will somehow triumph in the end."

—LISE HAND

MYTH NINE

"You are alone"

QUESTION: Are you sharing with others about your experience only to have them downplay it? Are they trivializing something that was very serious or harmful to you? Are they being compassionate for what your other must be going through? Are they saying such nonsense like at least you don't have children? Or worse, are they saying that's just how others behave in the mean time?

COACHING: Although you must do this yourself, you are not alone. Yes, you will discover that some of your closest friends and family think that supporting you means giving you their perspective on why you should consider yourself lucky or why the other may be behaving in such a manner. There is no trade for experience. They do not share your background of obviousness about the full spectrum of the other's irrational behavior. They can't possibly comprehend the truth without having experienced it first hand. They are innocently ignorant. Don't let them get away with such nonsense. Only you can correct such impotent wisdom. Speak up. Gently make sure they understand that they have no idea how hard this is for you and that they have no capacity to understand how threatening the other has been or is being to you or your children. Make sure they understand that not only are they not supporting you by being compassionate towards the other, but they are also actively shutting you down and silencing your voice by doing so.

This won't be easy, but it will be worth it. Healing requires you to speak up and share your voice aloud. You are hurting. You are the one who reached out to them for their understanding and compassion. Ask for what you need from them. You'll be surprised how clueless some of us are as how to support those we love in the mean time. We live in a cultural discourse that prefers listening to simple pleasantries over dark truths. You will need to fight the drift of suffering in silence and break the truth free. Name these irrational injustices aloud, even if others don't want to hear them or won't believe them. This is as much for them as it is for you. Getting your voice back, speaking the whole truth aloud is an essential part to your healing and effectiveness in climbing this mountain.

"There is no agony like bearing
an untold story inside of you."

—MAYA ANGELOU

MYTH TEN

"How I behave will impact how the other behaves."

QUESTION: Are you thinking that if you offer something, agree to something, then the other will be inclined to do the same? i.e. If you're amicable, they will be too. If you're hurtful, they will be too.

COACHING: The sooner you realize that nothing you do or don't do will affect the other's behavior either way, the better! Only they can alter their own behavior. Let me say that again. Only THEY can alter their own behavior. They are the ones who are choosing to be mean. You can count on them to keep behaving poorly. Think about it. Haven't you trained them that if they hold out long enough you will change your tune eventually?

*This is both sad news and liberating if you chose for it to be. If you truly accept that the other's behavior has nothing to do with yours, that they are going to chose for themselves either way, what do you have to lose?

*Bullies only stop when they are stood up to; face to face; with support from your attorney (the one with a noble soul). Never alone!

WORD OF CAUTION: Be prudent! As much as you can never fathom that the other may actually cause harm to you or your children, please listen and hear this! Take any and all appropriate precautions as if this could be a serious possibility. How many stories have we heard or read about where the spouse and/or children go missing and/or found dead? Too many! I'd rather you behave as such and not have needed to, than to be delusional and place yourself in serious harm. At the very least this means never, ever be alone with them again, ever! Always have someone with you other than the children, like a neighbor or a friend.

"It's not what happens to us, it is what we choose to do about what happens that makes the difference in how our lives turn out." —JIM ROHN

MYTHELEVEN

*"The injustice will be exposed and
retribution will be paid in full."*

QUESTION: Is your aim or goal for your ego to be intact
OR for you and your children to be intact... emotionally,
physically, academically, spiritually and financially?

COACHING: Fighting fairly means fighting in equal measure. If they are fighting for their full legal portion, than so
must you. If this is the case, you will need to fight for all of
it to walk away with the portion you will need to rebuild.
Negotiations will cut away from the whole, both sides. Only
you know what you need different from what you want.

Only you know what you can truly live with. Be satisfied with the actions and results you choose from unconditional love for yourself and for your children if you have children.

*At times it may feel like these choices are like losing a limb. Be satisfied it was just a limb and not you or the children.

WORD OF CAUTION: These sacrifices you make out of unconditional love for your children may be misconstrued and used against you as propaganda that you must have done something wrong or suspicious to be willing to agree to such a sacrifice on your part. This too may become part of the limb: falsely becoming persona non grata to some that you used to hold dearly in your heart. You may find that even after mustering the courage to reach out directly to some who mattered most, your character and credibility has been so destroyed by the other and their mastery in using specific truths out of context to paint a large falsehood, that the ones you reached out to will either not respond, give you a polite shove off or talk with you openly only later to be named on the other's witness list. The truth will have no chance to be set free with them. For the sake of your children, you will accept these losses.

On my path I courageously reached out to such individuals whom I loved dearly. All spoke caringly to me over the phone. I shared openly about the demise of our marriage, yet as cautiously as possible without speaking negatively about my other. Months later, when I received my other's list of witnesses, sadly three individuals were named as his witnesses, including the specifics of what two of them would testify to against me in Court. The heartbreak was excruciating. There was nothing I could do, but to accept these losses.

I must add here that if ever you find yourself knowing only one side of a story, especially if it is damaging to another's credibility, please be prudent before making any judgments, actions or conclusions. Please consider that you simply don't have enough to make an accurate assessment. A 'wolf in sheep's clothing' still looks like a sheep. Someone who is spreading such damage can actually be the perpetrator simply pretending to be the victim. They may harmfully slander the other for their own selfish gain and effectively cause damage to the other's reputation and relationships. It is a clever way for the perpetrator to use human nature to enlarge their support group and conceal their appalling deception to diminish the others. A scary example that I know about was when the other won the court battle and received full custody of their children. He later told them that their mother had sexually abused them as children, a complete and utterly false allegation, maliciously intended to cut her out of their life. It worked. Both her children and the new wife would only know his lies about her and believing them to be true, would not allow contact or communication with her. They would never know the truth and their mother would forever live with the inability to interact with her much loved children.

"*Remember if someone is talking about you behind your back, it just means you're steps ahead of them.*"

—UNKNOWN

MYTH TWELVE

"God will save you."

This is important. I invite you to use whatever best supports you to hear this wisdom. I'm aware that some of you may use other expressions to name a higher power, source, energy, etc...or you may have no such belief. All I ask is for you to consider that there are unseen forces that require no belief on your part yet still exist, such as gravity or the magnetic field that makes a compass always point North.

QUESTION: Are you steadily taking the steps you know to take or are you paralyzed in fear?

COACHING: God wants for you to have choice. God is with you and loves you, but like a great parent will NOT do it for you. God will help you when you ask; however, it may not look how you thought and wanted God's help to look. Only you have choice of your deliverance by your actions or inactions. How can you expect to be guided, sourced or energized if you are not climbing? Go through hell, don't stop and extend your visit!

You may be asking yourself what you did wrong. What possible karma payback is this? Here it is as simply as I can put it to help you best understand. This is part of an eternal back-and-forth struggle between light and dark. Consider that you have been shining your light so brightly that you are impeding upon the darkness. Perhaps you are even inspiring others to find and ignite their own light. You are therefore limiting the darkness and its territory. How strong is your faith? Will your light be extinguished? It will be tested. Are you willing to step into ongoing uncertainty believing that what you need, as you need it, will meet you at the appropriate moment? Will you endure until that moment arises? Will you continue to shine even in the darkest moments? Even when all seems lost and hopeless? You can if you dare to believe you can! Even in the mean time.

WORD OF CAUTION: You may have already fallen on your faith or had your light extinguished. You may have lost a battle along the way or done something seemingly unforgivable. It's never too late. Let me say that again. It's never too late. God still loves you. He is still with you even now when you may not feel it. He can move mountains, even yours! Forgive yourself now. Let it go now. Get back up now!

Now just so you don't go thinking that our own humanity won't fail us or that I'm flawless, here is my fall from grace. After trying to save my marriage for several years, when it was over, it was like a rubber band breaking. I had been stretching myself to accommodate Wahl's needs and not my own for so long that eventually I broke. I was done. The marriage was over and we were divorcing. I had spent the last four years approaching these terms so much so that when we were through, I was quite ready to move on. After we separated bedrooms and it was clear to one another that we were divorcing, I moved into another relationship. Since I knew the divorce would take some time to complete, I kept it private from everyone and intended to until we had separate households. As I shared before, the collaborative divorce process requires full disclosure. However, Wahl was behaving in a way that had me very skeptical about his true intentions, as he wouldn't come to agreement for me to move out and he wouldn't disclose his basic income financials, something the process called for and something I had been asking for for months, since the very beginning. My sense was to keep the details of just how romantic my involvement was close to my chest, but I did share openly that my heart had moved on, everyone knew.

About three months into the process, it was clear that the experts were questioning my credibility. My thought was that their perspective was that Wahl may be holding back his financial information because I wasn't disclosing my romantic details. It had been over 1 year now since we had declared our divorce and separated bedrooms and even the 4 experts involved couldn't get him to agree to give documented details of his income nor agree to let me move out using mother's financial support with no use of marital funds. So in urgency, thinking it may make the difference and regain credibility, I put together a communication including that my romantic involvement included the bedroom and the grounded reasons for not sharing before now for my attorney to read out loud to the other experts on their next conference call. I specifically asked her not to forward it, but to only read it to them aloud. I had already been assured by my clinical psychologist that any delicate matter would be handled together and discussed how best to share it with Wahl. So I was confident that at least the experts would know and we could discuss how best to share this news with him. After being asked how I wanted this shared, I told them that I would feel comfortable for Wahl to read it privately with his clinical psychologist at our upcoming meeting.

The response I received was that it was too late.

Completely against both my verbal and written requests, my attorney forwarded this communication to the entire collaborative team who in turn forwarded it directly to Wahl! So much for the 'collaborative' divorce process.

As you can imagine, I was immediately and totally in despair and misery, so much so that I couldn't drive. I wasn't home. My boyfriend was with me when I received this news as we had just attended a company meeting together with others. Seeing how utterly distraught I was, he offered to drive me home and then take a cab back to his car. I felt totally betrayed and was in overwhelming hopelessness and despair. Because knowing Wahl I knew this would be used as a heavy weapon against me. The very experts I hired to help me had just utterly and completely betrayed me. The person I was seeing took me home and I made the massive blunder of asking him to come in just long enough to hold me so I could try and rest and compose myself in time to pick up the kids from camp. As he intended to leave long before Wahl was to return, we didn't even bother to close my bedroom door.

The next thing we know we were awakened by yelling, with the door wide open, Wahl had come home early and was standing in the doorway to my room. He quickly left the doorway got to the staircase looked back, paused and smiled. I would later learn that he beat me in calling the collaborative team to reveal his version of what he had just witnessed. I hadn't imagined it getting worse and now this. I still have some unease when I think about this event. I have some in even writing this for you to read, yet I have a greater commitment to be honest with you as to the acute desperation you may feel and the support that you may need in the moment than I do to protect myself from embarrassment. It is more important for you to understand that it can be so great that it may lead you to take actions that are not in your best interest. Certain actions can betray you and your very purpose. Please know that I'm not proud of myself for this occurrence, yet it occurred over 1 year after declaring divorce, residing in separate bedrooms and separate levels of the house and trying for months to get Mr. Smiley's agreement to separate households. In hindsight I am now thankful that I wasn't alone when Wahl came home early that day, so early that I would not have left yet to pick up the kids from camp. I don't know what might have happened had I been home alone otherwise and why he came home early in the aftermath of having read the information his attorney had forwarded to him in such a blatantly reckless and irresponsible manner.

I immediately drove my boyfriend to the nearest store so he could call a cab and then went to pick up the children from camp. Wahl had already collected them. Apparently when he called the collaborative experts, they informed him that I was to stay in a hotel until our next meeting. He called me on the home line and left me this message and that I had 20 minutes to pack an overnight bag and get out of the house. At our next meeting scheduled within the week, I asked again to get his agreement to my separate residence that my mother would fund for me fully, again no marital funding required. Even in the face of these events, he still wouldn't give his agreement for me to move out.

No matter what you feel in such heated moments. Slow down and think. Remember urgency is a servant of the darkness. Please use your judgment and do not take any action that can potentially harm you even more. Yes, you may have a valid need to take such action, just don't! Be careful of YOU!

"The past is over. Forgiveness is giving up
all hope for a better past."

— JACK KORNFIELD

FINALE

Finally, please be gentle with yourself in the mean time. You are the best thing you still have. It will be necessary to give yourself gifts of scheduled down-time. Time to be still. Silence is golden. Time to rest. Time to eat. Time for simple pleasures. Watch comedies. Create humor. Laugh. A lot! Write. Be with nature. Pray or meditate. Listen to music. Move your body. Go for a walk. Dance. Love yourself. Pamper yourself. Get a massage. A mani/pedi. A small get-away. Rest. Eat. Visit friends and family or don't ~ whichever feeds your soul in the moment. These gifts will counter-balance the hard of the climb. For endurance and to reach the top, it is essential you keep balanced. Make no mistake; these pleasures are necessities, not luxuries! This too may be a new territory of learning for you.

Remember you are in the mean time. This is not an easy time. I promise it will pass. It will be worth it, but only if you dare for it to be. Try and fail, but do not fail to try.

Oh and lastly remember to breathe! The air can get pretty thin. It's especially the thinnest when you are closing in on your mountaintop. It can be done! Keep faith and take heart!

I leave you with the words of someone I consider to be a great example of lightness and wisdom.

"Today is your day. Your mountain is waiting.
Get on your way!" —DR. SEUSS

Best & blessings to you, my kindred spirits,

Toni

PRUDENT PRINCIPLES

Rather have them & not need them, than need them & not have them!

I recognize these principles will be too much information to take in all at once, yet I'd rather capture each one to their full extent, especially for re-reading. These are to serve you over time, not overwhelm you now! Instead, please treat yourself to one at a time, in loving spoonfuls. I trust you to be responsible for selecting the ones that empower you. Although the temptation may be strong, DO NOT hold these over you as a weapon, as something you already missed or should've been doing. I missed some of these myself. Please remember to be gentle with yourself. Let go of the ones that have already passed you by and empower yourself now with only the ones you can still do.

#1) PHYSICAL PRUDENCE: If you are still residing in the same household, do your best to never be in close proximity with the other. Also, try your best to always be on a level where there is an exterior exit! If you must, make sure you have taken precautions to ensure your safety no matter where you are in the house. Be prudent. Always be aware of your surroundings. Remember, you are in the mean time. Even a baseball bat can be better than nothing if you need it for protection. I'd prefer self defense training and pepper spray. Please trust yourself for what you and your circumstance need for protection. Don't worry if you feel foolish or even paranoid. Remember, I'd rather you have it and not need it, than need it and not have it. Please keep you and your children safe! Keep it legal. Keep it handy.

I privately bought a high strength door jam bar that I kept hidden in my room. No amount of force could bust through the door when it was wedged under the doorknob and against the floor. I would place it on my bedroom door when I went to sleep, as there was no exit on that level of the house. I also had an escape ladder, so I could go out my window if ever need be. If you are no longer in the same household, never be alone with the other ever again, including when with the children. If you must be in their presence, like at a sporting event for the kids, make sure there are several people around at all times. It's best to come with a friend or stay near someone you know. Let the other leave first. If you can't, than never isolate yourself from the crowd, like when walking to your car. Also take the time to train yourself in powerful self defense. Always keep your pepper spray, voice-recorder (see #3 below) and phone handy.

#2) A SUPPORT TEAM: You will need to make sure you have ample support in the following ways. This book and perhaps a mentor or coach who was successful in walking a similar journey to guide you along your way. A benefactor or another legal way to provide substantial financial means quickly. A select few companions and confidants who you can reach out to and lean on, whether by phone or in person who will be readily at your side for support, memory and optimism throughout your journey, like Samwise the Brave and the others were for Frodo Baggins. A positive atmosphere somewhere you can visit often for spiritual and personal growth. It may be a place of business like a coaching, fitness or wellness center, or it may be a place in nature or a religious house. There are a variety of uplifting places that will serve your body and soul in gaining strength for the climb. Pick and visit the ones that speak to you.

You will also need an experienced attorney who is licensed in your jurisdiction, has a noble spirit and is masterful at negotiating. Please have back-up support for care of your children for when you need a break. And finally there's YOU! You will be the constant and the one doing all of the work. Please pace yourself and use this team of support. You must also create and maintain a way to organize the myriad of required documents and collected data for your necessary divorce. It will serve for ease of access.

#3) TECHNICAL PRUDENCE: Find a safe computer elsewhere to do research. Even clearing history and searches may still be recoverable. Also please consider that all texts, emails, voice-messages and phone conversations can either be seen or overheard by the other. There is spy-ware. It is illegal, but the other is not interested in using this information in Court. The other can find valuable information to use against you, like overhearing what you are sharing with your family & friends or what your strategy is with your attorney.

Keep a video and voice recorder on you at all times. These are great tools to collect your own supporting documentation. They may also be used as a preventative measure just incase. I was unsure whether or not someone was going to harass me in public, if so I could easily pop out my voice-recorder, announce that I was now recording the conversation and perhaps that would be all it would take to have them leave me alone. It gave me comfort to know I had this handy if someday I needed it. Also, with a camera/video-recorder, I began documenting all activities I participated in with the children. I also took detailed photos of the marital house before I left yet after I removed my personal belongings, room by room, drawers & cabinets opened, so I could fully document the state of the house and all marital property w/date and time information as of the day I left. This became a great support to me for documenting the master list of all personal property to be equitably separated.

#4) BEFORE TAKING ANY DRASTIC ACTION, get expert legal advice from a competent attorney in your jurisdiction. For example, if you're thinking of leaving with the children, it may be possible for your other to sue for kidnapping, and you've just strengthened the case for the children to end up with the other. Also, if you're thinking of leaving without the children, you may be sued for abandonment, and you've just strengthened the case for the children to end up with the other.

For months, our collaborative divorce team had been trying to get agreement from Wahl to separate households. Once our marriage was declared over, he and I had separated into separate bedrooms. For over 1 year, we lived in separate bedrooms. However in my jurisdiction, separation required separate households, not bedrooms. Since we had children, we had to be in separate households for up to one year before we could even file for divorce. Even without using marital financial support, my other still wouldn't agree to it. When I finally moved out, it was against the collaborative process of mutual agreement yet with the encouragement from both collaborative divorce clinical psychologists. I was only permitted to take my personal clothing and belongings with me. Something as simple as taking furniture out of the marital home can be harmful to your case. No furniture. No small appliances.

I moved out one weekend while my other was away vacationing. My mom used what would've been my inheritance, a significant portion of retirement savings, to rent a separate residence AND furniture, including funding all living expenses for me and the children until I received temporary support from Wahl. She also paid for legal representation for almost two years. All of this in order for me to represent my case before a Judge and fight equitably for my legal portion to marital assets and custody of our children. It still took almost 6 months before the temporary support hearing (Pendente Lite hearing) where the Court ordered temporary alimony and child support to be paid. In one year alone legal services for my representation of the divorce cost over $70,000, of which about $20,000 was incurred for the production or collection of income from Wahl.

Yes sadly it's true, STILL in today's day and age. If you do not have the financial means to fight in Court, you have no option but to settle the divorce under your other's terms. Divorce is a domestic relations matter, not pro-bono work. The law requires you to prove your case in Court. If you have been cut off from your legal portion of your means, you have no ability to get to Court to prove it, ie. no case = no equitable justice. If you stand to fight for what's right, you must do so by finding alternate and significant financial means. Without my family's love and my mother's unreasonable financial generosity, my fight for what was right would not have been possible.

In my case it cost $25,000 to retain my noble attorney and another $25,000 for just 1 day in Court in my jurisdiction. The banks, mortgage and insurance companies will abide by their policies and procedures which honor the primary/owner account holder's instructions unless and until a Court orders otherwise. Words are insufficient to capture the harm, pain and expense incurred due to the simple fact that my other took the illegal and inappropriate actions which effectively cut me off from my legal portion of marital assets. Thank God for my mom! I count my family and their love among the top of my many blessings!

#5) LEGAL PRUDENCE: It will be your objective to obtain a successful, competent litigating attorney with a noble heart who is masterful at negotiating. They will ask for and earn your fee, and in equal measure they will have your best interest at heart. The gender of attorney does not matter here as much as their mastery in negotiations. In my experience alone, I've seen attorneys of both genders do a disservice to both their gender and their client due to their incompetence in powerful discernment and negotiation against gender bias and perception. I've also seen the opposite. Gender criterion alone is of no service.

It will also serve you to protect yourself and mitigate risk here as well. As such, you will also want to find the top 'asshole' lawyer in your jurisdiction. Your noble attorney will know 'the one'. You will want to remove them from any possibility in representing your other. This lawyer is only interested in lining their pockets with money. They are known to keep the divorce process going even when it could be resolved. Schedule a one hour consultation with them. Yes, this will cost you their consultation fee, but consider it an investment in removing risk. Once you consult with them, you will effectively create a conflict of interest, so this lawyer can no longer possibly represent your other.

WORD OF CAUTION: Beware of the collaborative divorce process. The team consists of an attorney and a clinical psychologist for each party, 6 persons altogether. It can only move forward if both sides come to mutual agreement. It requires full discloser, which means that there are no confidences kept between sides. This means the other side has the information that they would not otherwise gain in a confidential arrangement. The meeting minutes, documentation and emails CANNOT be used later in Court. The experts CANNOT testify to any details or exchanges in Court, other than that they represented the parties in their collaborative divorce. There is no right of discovery of evidence, subpoenas, etc...

If you have a scheming other, they may misuse this process unethically to buy time and reset the stage to their advantage. Wahl simply said the right things, completely denied or misrepresented true facts about us already agreeing to divorce back in the previous state and having been in discussions about it all for 10 months already. He knew these experts couldn't testify to what he had said later in Court, nor could the meeting minutes or emails be subpoenaed, so he could say whatever he needed to and get away with it. He did. His first question was whether or not the meeting room was bugged for recording our sessions? He then continued by saying that he had just found out I wanted a divorce and was dazed and confused. He looked like a grieving husband, earning the experts' compassion to take it slow due to his emotional state and readiness, yet never agreeing to anything other than what was in his gain alone, misusing this process for almost 1 year.

However, I agreed for him to set up a new banking account and agreed for him to get a new car for transporting the children, since the one he was using was the one my mom gave me and was just a two-seater. Any cash withdrawals I made from the joint account, I had to agree for him to receive the same amount in his account that I withdrew, even though he could withdrawal as much as he wished from his sole business account without repaying me. These agreements later backfired, as I couldn't undo them and once he decided to stop transferring money into the joint account and canceled our joint credit card, I had no access to funds. I had no way to identify how much he was now making, because the new income amount and information was now held in his new sole business account.

Later after I moved into another house, closer to Wahl's place of work for the sake of our children, he immediately began working from home and stopped traveling. Wahl wouldn't do either of these to save our marriage, yet he was able to do both immediately for the divorce. It was exposed months later that my other was getting coached by a litigating attorney throughout our collaborative divorce for almost 1 year, a violation unless disclosed to the team. It wasn't. My other said that he had only spoken to "a friend of his dad's", and saw no need to disclose this to the team. However, this 'friend' was his dad's attorney who later ended up representing my other as his litigating attorney in Court. With his attorney's help along the way, Wahl used the collaborative divorce process as a strategic maneuver to reset marital status quo and effectively removed me as our children's primary care giver before suing me for sole-custody in litigation.

For the first 8 years of their life, I was their primary caregiver. However in most jurisdictions, the Court considers more the most recent year of parenting as status quo and not the entire history of the marriage. I believe Wahl and his attorney's intention was to eradicate the year prior to this, where for 10 months of that year, I was the sole caregiver during the week while my other traveled out of state/out of country every Monday through Friday for work. With my other's new and improved parenting lifestyle, it soon became a fight for me to even have Joint Custody.

As you can imagine, I highly recommend AVOIDING the collaborative divorce process. The risk isn't worth it. Whether you are amicable or not, the litigation process is still better than the collaborative one and it requires mandatory mediation. In our jurisdiction it did, as well as allowing for discovery of evidence, which the collaborative divorce does not. If you both are truly amicable, then you will resolve your divorce in mandatory mediation and not get to Court. If your other is un-amicable, I strongly believe that the litigating divorce process is the ONLY process that will resolve the divorce. Think of it like using a hammer to drive in a screw. No matter how hard you try, no matter how experienced the handler, if you're using the wrong instrument, it simply won't work. Same with using the collaborative divorce process when one of you is a giver/sharer and the other is a taker/controller. You are gambling on the other to do the right thing, something they wouldn't even do to save the marriage. Why would they do so now in divorce? It's simply the wrong instrument for this dynamic of divorce and a colossal waste of time and money.

In my case it wasted 11 months and in excess of tens of thousands of dollars in marital assets simply to reset the stage to my other's advantage before litigating. Something my other could afford to do when I could not. The collaborative process only made it much worse for me. I had agreed to seemingly amicable agreements, yet in hindsight they were ridiculous. Once these agreements had me trapped in an irrevocable web and once he had the right amount of time being dad of the year, Wahl then stopped paying all invoices that were in my name only and cut me off from all financial means. He made it look like I had left him for another man and was now using our joint credit card recklessly. Instead I was attempting to avoid him ruining my credit and because no other financial means were available to me, I had no choice but to use it to pay past due services to my attorney including all late fees, since he had stopped paying these invoices himself. Meanwhile, he spent in the neighborhood of $10,000 on a new puppy and a new invisible fence. He sued me for sole custody, all marital property and assets, and even his legal fees. He sued me for everything knowing I would have no financial means to fight our divorce in Court which now included his accusation of adultery, which ultimately had no sustenance and therefore was absent in the final divorce decree.

Stay away from the collaborative divorce process!

#6) FINANCIAL PRUDENCE: First, do your best to know and locate every financial account (sole or joint) you and the other have, the bank/institution(s), the account number(s), and the most recent statement. Don't forget copies of all previous tax returns and any income statements. Please include all checking accounts, savings accounts, business ac-

counts, credit card accounts, investment accounts, brokerage accounts, 401k accounts, Roth IRAs, Traditional IRAs,
life insurance cash value accounts, etc... If you are not the
primary on your joint checking or savings accounts or if you
are not the one managing the finances or the online banking BEWARE! My other managed our finances and was the
primary on all checking, savings accounts and life insurance
policies. Without cause or my agreement, my other placed
'pass-codes' on all of our joint accounts, both banking and
brokerage, during the collaborative divorce process. The
team of 4 professionals could do nothing about this, as they
held no authority over us. Even though I was legally named
as joint and the account was still open, this simple maneuver
not only cut me off from any and all access to the funds in
the account, but it also cut me off from any and all history,
including statements.

However, joint brokerage accounts are treated differ-
ently. Either party at any time can move all assets from a
joint brokerage account into their own private account without the other parties' knowledge or permission. I noticed
my other stopped paying invoices that were in my name
only, including to my collaborative divorce attorney. At our
meetings and in the presence of our collaborative team, my
other repeatedly told us he would pay these. After receiving late fees and collection agency notices, in self-defense
and to preserve my good credit, as I already mentioned, I

withdrew funds from our joint brokerage account to pay for these known past-due invoices since my other wouldn't take the appropriate, agreed upon action. This was the action he claimed justified shutting me off from my portion of marital funds. In an instant I no longer had access to my legal right of my portion of marital funds.

When it came time to present our expenses in Court, I didn't have evidence to show his income nor our expenses in all our years of marriage. It forced me to spend even more money to get a Court Order to subpoena his workplace and the financial institutions for this information, as well as manually track what my current expenses were for me and our children for the next 6 months now in a separate residence. The amount of expense, time and energy this took was ridiculous, as well as the fact that our living expenses drastically reduced to the bare necessities as my family was now funding me & the children's living expenses, as well as my legal fees. This was also to my other's advantage significantly reducing what would be considered status quo expenses, so legally speaking the amount of spousal and child support would now be based on these un-equitable, significantly reduced figures. My monthly support for the children became less than 10% of Wahl's monthly income.

#7) POST-DIVORCE PRUDENCE: I recommend as part of your Custody Agreement to try and capture all agreements clearly, leave no room for interpretation. Also, try and make all hand-offs of children to and from school or camp. Consider including in your Custody Agreement an agreement to hire and work with a Parent Coordinator.

A Parent Coordinator is a licensed clinical psychologist who is trained to work with families and children in divorce. They will serve to facilitate meetings between you and your other to discuss and coordinate action between you both regarding the children. A Parent Coordinator will not usually meet the children, unless necessary. They represent neither of you and there will be no confidences kept; however as part of their agreement, you both will sign a release so they can testify under oath as to their expert opinion and experiences with both parties in front of a Judge for any future Court hearing such as a Custody Re-modification. Please be clear, this professional will not serve to help you as in therapy or in changing your behavior with one another. However, a Parent Coordinator will serve to support you by facilitating discussions, having an expert witness to document meetings, threats, violations and concerns. I don't like to be the bearer of bad news, but if you are beginning to think that it will stop after the divorce is final or after they've moved on with another, please think again. Remember, my intention is to lovingly place you on solid ground for your own good!

One such example after my divorce was about the children's doctors. Since having lived in this area for the previous years, we were already established with their pediatrician and dentist. My suspicion however was that given all appointments and history with these doctors were with me only, he was attempting to systematically remove them as their physicians. He would eliminate the true history of our family and only experience him as the now involved dad, since he was now coming to their appointments. After sharing this information with the Parent Coordinator, she told him not to take our child to this new doctor for his annual visit, just for his sickness instead. My other ignored her altogether and did both. At our next meeting, our Parent Coordinator looked my other in the eye and told him that she had officially flagged his file as 'going rogue' and if ever she was to testify before a Judge in the future she would inform the Judge of her professional opinion and this finding directly. Needless to say, it was decided that we remain with the same pediatrician.

Having this professional when you are dealing with your other is better than having no one, especially when dealing with someone who controls by consistently being tardy, coming un-prepared like without their calendar for scheduling the next meeting, not honoring agreements, deliverables and/or deadlines, or even overstaying their welcome. Parent Coordination is a key for having any chance to coordinate co-parenting activities and events for the children, including extra curricular sports and birthday parties.

#8) SPIRITUAL PRUDENCE: There will be times along your journey when you have no way of seeing your way through. These are the moments you will find hardest to summon your faith, take heart and keep going. It was as if just when I needed it most, I would hear a song or a stranger would comfort me with care by saying the exact right words. I would see a license plate or read a book and hear the wisdom that struck a chord in my spirit and would give me goose-bumps. The quotes you've read at the end of the myth chapters were some of mine. I trust that these too will arise for you in the moments when you need them most. Keep an eye out for them. Goosebumps may also be your experience when they arrive. They will serve you.

One that supported me greatly was an excerpt from Paulo Coelho's book *Aleph*. I came across this part in his book which captured in words all that I couldn't say for myself and my own mean time journey. Ultimately I read it as a prayer of forgiveness for all of it: for the journey, all of its participants and all of its outcomes. Here it is for you in the hopes that you too may be served by reading this. If you are in a place where you can, I recommend reading it aloud.

"Hilal searches for inspiration on the golden walls, the columns, the people coming at this hour of the morning, the flames of the lit candles.

- I forgive the girl I was, not because I want to become a saint but because I do not want to endure this hatred. This tiresome hatred.

This was not what I expected.

- You may not forgive everyone and everything, but forgive me.

- I forgive everything and everyone. I forgive you because I love you and you do not love me. I forgive you because you reject me and I am losing my power.

She closes her eyes and raises her hands towards the ceiling.

- I am liberated from hatred by means of forgiveness and love. I understand that suffering, when it cannot be avoided, helps me to advance towards glory.

Hilal speaks softly but the acoustics of the church are so perfect that everything she says seems to echo throughout the four corners. But my experience tells me that she is channeling the spirit of a child.

The tears I shed, I forgive.
The suffering and disappointments, I forgive.
The betrayals and lies, I forgive.
The slandering and scheming, I forgive.
The hatred and persecution, I forgive.
The punches that were given, I forgive.
The shattered dreams, I forgive.
The dead hopes, I forgive.
The disaffection and jealousy, I forgive.
The indifference and ill will, I forgive.
The injustice in the name of justice, I forgive.
The anger and mistreatment, I forgive.
The neglect and oblivion, I forgive.

The world with all its evil, I forgive.

She lowers her arms, opens her eyes and places her
   hands on her face. I move closer to kiss her,
   but she makes a signal with her hands.

- I have not finished yet.

She closes her eyes and looks up.

Grief and resentment, I replace with
   understanding and agreement.
Revolt, I replace with music that comes from my violin.
Pain I replace with oblivion.
Revenge, I replace with victory.

I will be able to love above all discontentment.
To give even when I am stripped of everything.
To work happily even when I find myself in
   the midst of all obstacles.
To dry tears even when I am still crying.
To believe even when I am discredited.

She opens her eyes, puts her hands on my head and
   says with an authority that comes from above:

- Thy will be done. Thy will be done."

ACKNOWLEDGEMENTS

This book is dedicated to my family, friends, and all who stood by me and carried me through my own mean time journey. I dedicate this book to those in my village.

Clarence A. McGillen, III, my inspiring and loving husband. You are my rock, my protector, my love, my best friend and soul mate all wrapped into one. I only wish there were more of you in the world for deserving women who want to feel what it is like to be loved entirely for who they truly are, flaws and all.

My children. Although you had nothing to do with what happened between your father and I, still you played a special part in this journey. For without you, I wouldn't have found the purpose, strength and passion that was worth enduring all that came with doing what was in the highest and best interest for you. A mother's love can be truly inspiring, even to me. My proudest accomplishment is being your mom!

SL & RW, my beautiful, generous and loving mom & step-dad. You are the truest example of what being the best mother in the world is. You are my hero, my biggest fan, and my first experience of unconditional love.

BT & MT, my loving and proud dad & step-mom. Thank

you for being my dad and for standing up for your little girl. Saying what needed to be said, when the time had come to say it. May daughters across the world feel what it's like to have parents stand up for and love them the way you've done for me.

To both sets of my parents: I love that you each found one another and a love that you truly deserve. I celebrate having you all as my parents.

TT, KJ, and EP, my original BFFs and sisters. Thank you for being by my side through all of my life's journeys. It's a blessing to have beautifully different, powerful women as my sisters. Each with her own values and village, brought together by God in this beautiful tapestry of sisterhood. Together we are a blessing to one another like no other, none alike, but all with an amazing heart and soul.

HH, my noble attorney and champion. You are the best example I've encountered of mastery and integrity in your profession. You were exactly what was needed along this journey. Thank you for being with me and effectively advising me in and through the mean time. I am honored to know you.

JB, my courageous wing woman and dear friend. I pray you never experience what it took for me to fully understand what a true friend is. To be willing to fly cross-country at a moment's notice, having your children cared for by others, so you could be with me in my hour of need. To set the record straight even if it meant putting yourself in the middle to do what you knew in your heart to be right. I am delighted to spend the rest of my life thanking and cherishing you, even when you insist I already have done it enough.

NV, my generous friend and kindred spirit. Having traveled a similar journey, you reached out and ask what I really needed and didn't take 'I don't know' for an answer. For you to have understood fully without me having to say much, I was beyond grateful. As long as I exist, you will always know what it means to have someone in your corner with loving arms and an open heart.

To my extended family, my lifetime friends, my accomplishments, my hidden heroes, my heartaches, my failures, and my self chosen adversaries, welcomed or not, you have each touched my life and by doing so created me. You've been essential to my life. I share this book for the difference it can make for others in the mean time and for their children and families. For those, like Don Quixote from Man of LaMancha, who are dreaming the impossible dream, fighting an unbeatable foe, bearing with unbearable sorrow, running where the brave dare not go by using their last ounce of courage to reach the unreachable star. I also dedicate this book to YOU.

Carpe Diem

TONI McGILLEN, PCC, NCOC

Toni McGillen is a Professional Certified Life Coach,
and is designated as a PCC credentialed coach by the
International Coach Federation (ICF). She is a certified
graduate of Newfield Network's accredited coach training
program and has her own coaching practice. She has
been coaching since 1997. Toni has also worked in the cor-
porate arena as an Industrial Engineer for both American
Express and McNeil Consumer Products. Toni graduated
magna cum laude with her Bachelor Degree from Arizona
State University in Industrial Engineering. Toni became
successful in her field, yet chose to be out of the workforce
and with her children at home while they were young.

Made in the USA
Columbia, SC
20 February 2018